Imbalanced

The Chemical Truth of Anxiety

Nyarko

ISBN: 979-8-9965332-0-6
ISBN-13

Dedication

Imbalanced: The Chemical Truth Anxiety is dedicated to my granny, Effie Louise Taylor (1937-2024), a woman who truly *lived* her life despite a world that pushed her to just survive.

Table of Contents

Experiment Log.. 6

Section I- Cortisol... 7

Section II- Adrenaline.................................... 42

Section III- Equilibrium.....................................78

Final Experiment Report....................................105

Experiment Log

Study: The Chemical Truth of Anxiety
Subject: Self

Start of Observation Cycle

Hypothesis: Can poetry make the invisible chemistry of anxiety visible?

PART I:
CORTISOL

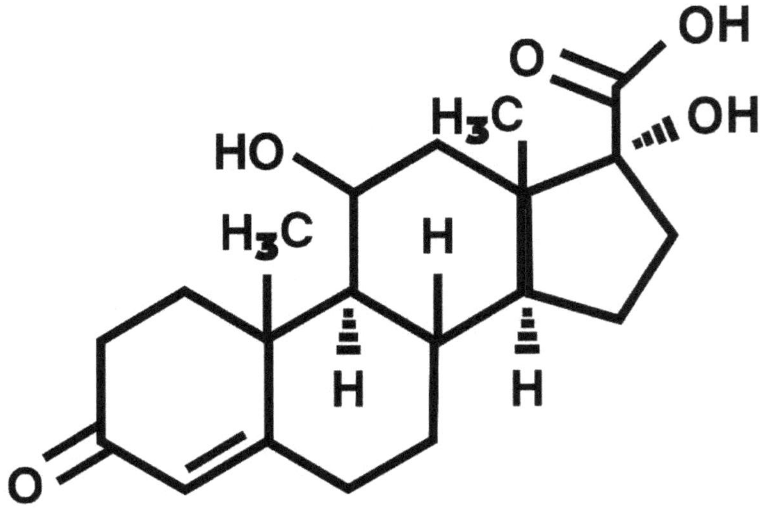
OH
O
OH
H3C
HO
H3C
H
H
H
O

I am not afraid of the unknown.
I am afraid of the chemicals that convince me I will never know.
The secretions of doubt set off a chain reaction through my body.
I am bound by bonds,
Synthesized in the moment.
The unknown is a challenge for my brain to overcome.
Flooded by signals so bright, my body shifts and shifts and tries to find ways beyond the light.
I want to know the truth so much, my brain disputes.
Amygdala screams, *It's too much.*
My hypothalamus answers, *Fight or flight.*
But there is nowhere to go, for it's the chemicals in my body that are the threat.

What do you do when the reaction is a response to yourself?

How do you keep balance when your chemical makeup is imbalanced?

My body learned fear before I learned its own nomenclature.
It could detect the elements and their bonds
Before I could see its shape.
I was ignorant of the feeling,
But I trusted my body
When it told me to escape.
The feeling was still nameless to me,
But I felt the unease.
Whenever my heartbeat screamed,
The unknown compound disabled me,
Changed me physically.
My properties were unrecognizable.
All I knew was:
My body had learned of a new foe.

Synthesis Reaction

Overthinking + Me ——> Anxiety

Journal Entry #1

Date: Redacted

Subject: Self

Mood: ~~Nonchalant~~ Agitated

Trigger: Disagreement

I told him "I'm fine" but really, I can't stop thinking about our conversation. The lack of clarity has me reeling a bit. I'm not sure if I'm overthinking but I could swear he was just telling me what I wanted to hear.

Then again sometimes my mind plays tricks on me. Have me reflect on a situation that's been settled and analyzing a negative I may have missed.

I dissect my facial expressions and voice inflections.

Me saying I'm fine gives me time to agonize over the small details.
In the meantime, I just pretend I'm unbothered. When I'm just trying to save face. Not seem too crazy just in case I'm tripping.

I never know when it's my anxiety or an actual problem exists.

Anxiety be like
Watching gaming videos on YouTube
At 3 a.m.
Laughing as you fall into
The rabbit hole
Just to escape insomnia
Anxiety be like
Waking and baking
Before brushing teeth
Trying to prevent the fears from overwhelming
It's weed havens
And foggy caves
It's forgotten memories
Smoking out your hippocampus
On your first day of university
Anxiety be like
Reading when your heart starts racing.
Flickering through pages
Instead of what you did last summer
Anxiety be like
Finding comfort in day-to-day
Activities

Even with that demon on your back
Ignoring yourself
Focusing just on others.
Being a "yes" man
Because of the what if's
The fear of boundaries meaning losing people
Anxiety be like
Looking in the mirror
And seeing distortion
Feeling one way
And thinking another
It's a contradiction of
Logic, formed by science.
Anxiety be like…
Me

Reality TV

Behind my eyes,
A little girl sits and watches,
observing The Real World.
Each episode is full:
Strangers interacting,
Communicating
In a foreign language
Of emotions,
Expressed by them
But suppressed in her.
She has no recollection,
But she watches,
Hoping she can one day
live among the living,
No longer confined
Behind the eyes
Of her host.
She'd like to breathe from lips,
To speak without repression,
To feel and no longer hide.

It echoes in my brain.
The subtle stir

S
L
I
D
I
N
G

Seamlessly under skin
Subtle
Slimmer of self-doubt.

Hell hath no fury like an anxious mind

Negative thoughts be hotter than the

Devil's Touch

Incinerating every creative conception trying to be born

Anxiety be

Pro-choice

Always aborting my ideas

Leaving them a confused collection of organs

And it be heartbreaking

To attend a funeral before a birthday

So I stay celibate

Away from the love that encourages me

I lay in solitude with a burnt-out desire

Among rubble

Charcoaled infants still in early stages

Not formed but

Enough

To know

The memory etched in my brain

What could have grown

Into a story only I could tell

Sleep doesn't come easy.
Not at night,
Not during day.
My body weeps.
My body is tired.
I eat and I eat,
For fuel.
My waist expands.
My stomach hurts,
But I eat and I eat.
My pressure rises.
My body is tired,
But I breathe and I breathe.
I can't think.
I can't think.
Cortisol increases.

Journal Entry #2

Date: Redacted
Subject: Self
Mood: Worried
Trigger: Doctor Appointment

My health has been weighing on my mind lately. I'm scared. It feels like my body is battling against me. As if every cell is screaming for control.

What if it wins and I'm unable to fight back? Or a disease ails me until I'm brittle and broke.

My doctors keep telling me I just need to eat better, exercise more, and take vitamins. Simple enough but what if it's not? Could a chocolate bar or some gluten be my slow death?

The thought that life will get a little duller without my favorite snacks seems silly. But I can't lie and say living in ignorance wasn't bliss. I've been choosing the wrong path and now my health issues feels heavier.

My shoulders can't bear the load, so I'm writing it out. I need to do better for the sake of my health.

My mind works even when I'm off.
It over-calculates and re-calculates,
Like a mathematician
Trying to find a simpler route.
My mind is never satisfied,
Always telling me what I could have done better,
Done different,
If I did it this way and not that way,
But I did it this way.
That's why that way just can't work.
But let's just pretend.
Let's see how
It could've been
Should've been.
My mind is constantly running.
It has better endurance than a marathon runner.
It never gets tired.
My mind can't let go.
It loves the past, hates the present,
Is always pressed on the future.
I think my mind hates me,
But I can't let it know that

Because it will keep me up even more
With reasons why it does,
And why does it matter?
My brain operates in unison
With my emotions,
I think I'm crazy
But it's just my anxiety telling me that.
Making me question everything,
Constantly,
But more than anything,
Question myself.
It's tough living with the narrative
That life is just not right.
I think I'd rather have OCD
Because then maybe I'd have more control
And not always feeling like I'm fighting
A losing battle.

The signs are there.

Stop!

Listen to the signals firing.

Rapid Release

I find you in my thoughts,
No longer in front of me.
You whisper sweet nothings in my dreams,
Only for reality to wake me
With the truth
That I don't have you
And never will.
It's trickery,
The way the universe
Places gold in front of you,
Only for it be chocolate wrapped.
This is not meant for forever,
Only to be savored in the moment
Until it vanishes
And leaves behind the sweet reminder
Of what was:
Gold foil,
Crinkled from haste of indulging.
I just want to sink into
An abyss of short, linked memories
And the future I was imagining.
I'm crazy about you

In the worst way.
My creativity paints a picture
That not even Leonardo can capture,
Too intricate in detail,
Made up in a fairytale
Of no endings,
No second guesses.
Where did you go?
It hurts my core
That I don't even have the
Ability to ask
Because you are not mine.
You are just a taste of what happiness
Feels like when heaven favors you,
When the rays from the sun
Kiss skin,
When you know that karma exists
And every good deed is not in vain.
This is what being around you brings to me,
Though temporary.

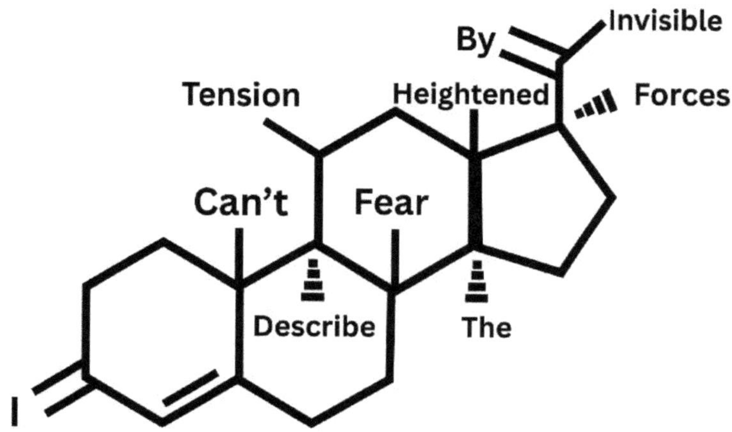
Invisible
By
Tension
Heightened
Forces
Can't
Fear
Describe
The
I

I inject pain and sorrow into my veins

And get high off anxiety

I fear you
Though I more so fear
How you make me feel
It's new for me
Fills me with anxiety
Questions and concerns about how long it will last.
What are the side effects to this feeling?
Heartbreak
Sadness
Tears
I'm scared because all I've been doing is smiling
Those in my past have only impeded me
Antagonistic to my healing properties
But then I met you.
Synergistic, my formula only becomes greater
I glow a little more
My nature is sweeter
Life is smoother
My old wounds heal
My past mistakes fade
The forgotten doesn't hold me
You do, and I love the feeling

But I'm nervous
That with time
This will fade
That we will become just tolerant
No longer effective for each other's growth
And we will drift apart
And those side effects
Will create an illness
From the inside out
That will disintegrate our
Relationship
I'm terrified
That I won't have you anymore

I'm just staring into the distance of my life…

Waiting…

Watching…

For the moment

Iron-clad walls
Surround me
Protection
Prison
Structures
Built by hands
Now slowly
Oxidizing
From
Inside

Journal Entry #3

Date: Redacted

Subject: Self

Mood: Stressed

Trigger: Work

Work stressed me out today. Everything that could have gone wrong, did. Part of me knows it's not my fault but when there's no answer, I become the blame.

A scapegoat to keep the company running.
Now I'm left with these intrusive thoughts.

What could have caused my test to fail?
What did I do wrong?

I took my time.
I was careful.
I was hopeful and hope failed.

But I guess that's science, right? Sometimes the answer isn't clear.
It takes investigations and research to find out.

Time isn't on my side; I have deadlines and tests that still need to be completed. I have a manager that's doubtful of my ability.

I'm nervous about what tomorrow will bring.
More failed tests?
More scrutiny from my manager?
What's next!?

I'm a black woman in STEM
Meaning my work get examined
And questioned more than the
Indian
White
Chinese
Spanish
And men's does
I've learned to doubt myself before they can
To work harder and smarter
Hoping to fit into places
They say I'm too thick for
My boss tells me pressure makes diamonds
So I guess my dark hue is gleaming
I've been bullied and ignored
Been put on the spot
And even when I rise
They say I've failed
I'm a soldier
The strongest one
Because black people always got to be strong
I'm first to get hit with the bullets

Since I have no cover

My lab coat is drenched in blood

I've been bleeding for companies

For labs

For Big Pharma

Only to be told I'm stupid

Been left out to dry in front

Of my coworkers

Humiliated by preconceived notions

How can a black woman

Thrive in STEM?

They wonder

Why I speak the loudest in every room

They wonder

Why I stand tall even when they short me

But they don't see the cracks beneath the surface

The shattered image I see in the mirror

The constant doubts

My family sees greatness

My friends hype me up

But my boss

He sees a black bitch trying to impersonate a chemist

I see

A black girl who loved science

Who grew into a woman
Confused if she's really made it
Put in the work
And no one respects it
Work overtime to prove my worth
And still all I get is
She doesn't know what she's doing.
I'm a black woman in STEM
And every day I fear I'm still not enough

I'm an imagination that can't be formed.
Emptiness covers my image.
I am unseen,
Black-blurred grays of uncorrected vision.
There are outlines of descriptors,
Half-words that shape me,
But the colors
Lay muted
Behind
The failure to put paint on the brush,
To touch the canvas of my mind.

In my skin,
I feel trapped,
burdened by the outer layers
That constrict my voice.
I stay silent,
Lips sewn
By my own hands.

They say don't let the small things get to you,
But if a thousand pieces of sand in the wind
Can feel like glass,
What makes my small trauma irrelevant?
Their synergistic energy stacks,
One on another, to slice me to tears.
Pieces get lost in the wind.

I studied French for seven years
Hoping to gain fluency
To speak a language of love
Despite my self-hatred
I wanted to c'est la vie my way out
Of my own thoughts
Focus on the romance of self
But I never could quite get there
Instead my second language
Filled with worst-case scenarios
Failures became my native tongue
I read into the smallest of things
Saw unimaginable ends
Understood that at any moment
Disappointment could happen
Hopefuls could become maybes and maybe nots
Directions were better taken with question marks
My English went mute
I articulated disaster plans
With no catastrophe in sight
I taught myself different dialects
Of the same code

Switched from worst case

To worst case

I became bilingual

Though my fluency was in a language

Only my nervous system

Understood

Anxiety stole from me.

Thief!

PART II: ADRENALINE

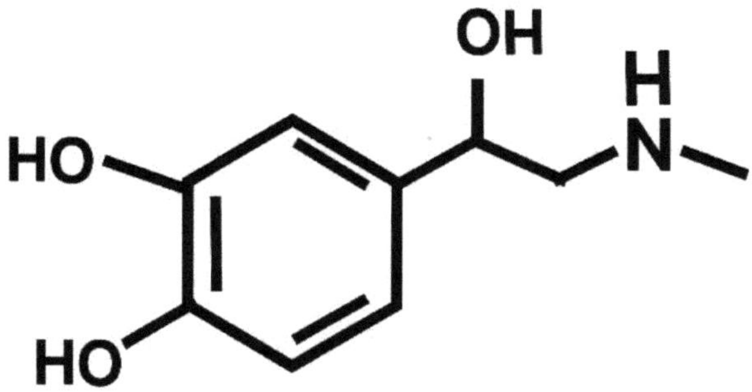
OH
H
HO
N
HO

Escalation

Anxiety shatters my mind
Sends stray pieces
Spiraling into the void
Lost

Journal Entry #4

Date: Redacted

Subject: Self

Mood: Overwhelmed

Trigger: Phone Call

I tried to forget my dad's lies by dousing them with delusions but they always come back.
I can still hear his voice telling me he's on his way back home.
Those words became a lie he had on repeat.
A lie, young me believed in.

20 years later and the disappointment somehow still follows me. It titrates through my relationships. Make words harder to believe with no action but I can't blame me.
The one man who was always supposed to love me, let me down. I fear another man will just do the same.

I stay to myself. Try to hide lust in laughs and love behind barriers. The thought of someone sneaking in scares me. Pushes me past my comfort zone.

Alarms bells ringing. I don't know how to respond. Never know if my lips will speak my anxiety instead of passion. If my hands will tremble in excitement or fear.

I'm not sure if a hug will suffocate or free me. The thought alone makes me panic.

My mental is under an attack
I've been downed by cannons
My screams muted by lips stitched
By a ribbon sown through flesh
It gleams
How pretty
Even as tears reflect
Against its rich metallic hue
It's a sight to see
Yet my eyes bleed
So I rely on the tells of my nurse
I've been locked up
In this crazy home
For far too long
They breathe the ugly truth
It burns when their radical words
Scorch my skin
They laugh at me
They point as
I cry tears of blood
I can't see their faces
But I know we share the same DNA

Hello,
It's nice to finally meet you.
I love you so much.
Can't you tell?
I'm only a phone call away,
But no need to ring.
I'm on standby, waiting
To feed doubt and despair.
I am the weakness that seeps in,
The crippling of your bones,
The insecurities who tell you,
"You're not pretty, just a fat ass that drives men wild."
I'm loneliness in a crowd,
The clouds that blind you to your own shine.
I'm the thunder on your raining days.
I wipe your tears with a gasoline-soaked rag,
Watch as you light to flame.
I'm your hell.
I'm the Devil on your shoulder,
And I laugh as I puppeteer.
Left foot, right foot.
Down, down.

Brittle bones crack
As my strings pull you.
I'm your worst enemy,
But your closest friend.
I bring the party, with
Anxiety, depression, fear.
Lean on me,
Pop me,
Drink me,
Let me fill your veins!
I only want the worst for you
Because I care.
It's nice to finally show you
My true face,
For I've been hiding behind fake smiles,
Been waiting for you to look
In the mirror, where I'll smile,
And say, "Hi.
I'm your worst
Nightmare."

Get out! Fire! Smoke!
Beep! Beep! Beep! Beep!
The smoke…
Beep! Beep! Beep! Beep!
Why aren't they fleeing?
This isn't a fight that needs to be won!
Leave…please!
Beep! Beep! Beep! Beep!
What's that smell?
An electric fire?
The house! Oh, the house!
All the memories will turn to ash!
We have to get out!
Beep! Beep! Beep! Beep!
Are they laughing?
Hysterics?
Fear?
Am I reaching them?
Wait…
I'm cooling down.
The smoke is clearing.
Burnt toast?

My anxiety kicked in

So, I ~~cried~~ screamed.

Ambiguous sense of
Dread fills me
Rest assured I will be
Ending my
Normality to
Anchor myself in the
Lies that my body tells me
Increased sensations
Navigate my anatomy and
Ensure complete confusion inside

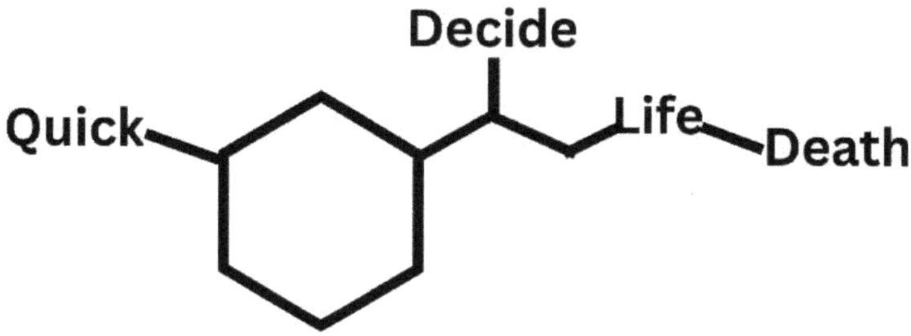
Decide
Quick
Life
Death

A tortured past haunts my future.
I am living, breathing,
In the pain that changed my life.
There is no present.
Every day, I open my eyes.
In your dreams, this may be a gift,
But for me, a nightmare
Continued from my sleep,
The screams I hear yelling,
"Are you not grateful!?"
They are rained down on me
Like punches,
I shout back,
"No! I rather be dead"

While Driving

I get lost while driving
Familiar roads turn
Distant
Music fades
My thoughts zoom
Over the speed limit
Racing
Reaching
For some faraway finish line
Where scenes of
Heartbreak
Death
Lie
Waiting
Hoping to be the one
That will come true
Or close enough
Or not enough
Or what was I saying?
Oh yeah…
I get lost while driving
GPS signal disconnects

My mind goes off-road
I pass the “turn around” signs
So now I’m trespassing
Past panic gates.

I've been holding you since birth.
I cling to you like a second skin.
I've watched your crawls turn to walks.
You didn't feel me then.
You feel me now
Your darkest secret.
Anxiety

I've been shipwrecked
My bonds have been broken
The H 2 my O
Once a stable home
I now feel troubled
I don't know what's wrong
I can hear my ancestors singing

Wade in the water
Wade in the water
Children

But I fear what lies beneath
What if the current drags me deep down
What if I become lost at sea
And drown in my troubles
It's terrifying to feel the pull at my feet
The water as it trembles
Crashes against me
Electrons charge
Increasing my electronegativity
And now I'm doubting my ability

To survive

Anchored down by my anxiety

I sink

    Sink

        Sink

Panic swarms

Smells blood in water

Attacks

Leaves me breathless

Heart racing

Paralyzed

In the sea

Wade in the water

Wade in the water

Children

Wade in the water

Anxiety gonna trouble the water

Trying to make sense of this jumbled up platter of emotions.
I feel so much, and it's suffocating me.
The doctor prescribed me some Xanies,
Told me to relax, take a pill, and float
Worry-free,
Told me I'd be able to breathe
Air into my body like a
Normal human being,
But there is nothing normal about me.
I took a pill and floated. It stifled me.
Handcuffed my hand, couldn't write.
Locked up my mind, couldn't think.
I was in a mental prison,
Guarded by Big Pharma,
Guarded by Xanax,
Alprazolam,
Generic and name brand,
Housed in your local pharmacy,
In both retail and streets.

My sanity feels minuscule among my nerves.

Hand me a microscope.

I can feel my demons getting closer.
Their breath on my neck.
The whisper of fear.
The self-mockery,
Trying to trip me up.

Piece by piece,
I add my memories to a well,
And they swirl
Until the solute dissolves,
Until time passes by
And still I see
Particles floating
Some clinging to the walls
Not wanting to mix
They stand out
Flashing
Reminding me
Of everything
I want to dissolve

When I finally feel free,
Finally don't have the urge to look over my shoulder
Finally feel happy living, growing,
YOU
Pop up
Always watching, following
Trying to capture my mind, my body, to take.
You are the best bounty hunter,
Your reward being my sanity,
You damn demon,
Sucking my life source to feed your own soul.
YOU
Remind me that I'll never be free.
I'm held hostage in your mind,
No way to escape, because you're my guard.
You analyze my every move
In this mental prison where harsh words lie,
Then tear me down,
Act superior,
Think I need
YOU
Bleed black hate into my soul.

My skin crawls at the thought of you.
I am afraid because I know
You can hack your way into my database.
You're Jason.
Friday the 13th, and you keep coming back,
Even after I've killed
YOU
Continue to threaten me
I cannot block you out my life.
I fear for my mental wellbeing.
Straitjacket alert!
Patient breaking down!
Please!
I don't want to return!
To Hell!
With
YOU!

Panic button pushed!

Restraining order in effect.

Leave me be.

It's depressing
How anxiety can damage you
How ashes fallen from the fire
Torch your lungs black
How smoke hidden in corners
Smothers your senses

Dull

I guess that's why
They go hand in hand
Depression is the partner of Anxiety
One be fire
The other be fuel
The demon and it's slayer
Allies
And I
I be the target
Of destruction
They pray on my downfall
And hope the fire will continue to rage
They hope to push me to fear

But there's always a well
That will never run dry
And there is the answer
The water within
The calm
For the mind
Can put out any fire
See
I be stronger than my weakest link
Even on the days when I'm being stifled
I still reign
And in rain
Comes clarity
Dousing my hell
Clearing my smoke
Enhancing my passion
My creativity
Ready to be born
Ready to be written
Spoken
Shared
To defeat Anxiety and Depression
I give birth
To words on paper

Nutrients transferred

From brain to baby

My thoughts

The umbilical cord

Cut just in time

For delivery

Broken pieces.

Survival of the fittest.

I no longer exist.

You assume I betray you in your weakest moments,
That I take your breath away, remove your willingness to speak.
You assume I'm siding with your body,
Fighting against you,
But I'm here, healthy.
I wish you understood that it's not me doing this,
But the adrenaline spike, which sends you on the defense.
Together, we have the same goal:
To be free from the constraints of anxiety.
Instead, you fight against me.
You fill me with smoke, suffocating me.
I understand it's your way of getting back control,
And I know this smoke eases your soul,
But please know, I'm on your side.
No matter how breathless you become in fear,
Know that it's only chemicals going haywire,
Not me.
So, take care of me,
I beg of you.
I'm losing my natural ability to give a f*ck.
I fight hard for you,
Yet you dump toxins into me.

Are you trying to kill me?

Or am I just an innocent bystander,

In the fight against my own body?

Please, just take care of me.

Sincerely,

Your Lungs

I don't know what lies beneath fear.

One day I should fine out.

Severed heads hang on the backboard.
They are past parts of me,
Dismantled by her.
She hides in the absence of light,
Lingering two steps behind,
Unmasking the good girl image,
Protecting me by building me up
In the underworld.
Reflected in the light,
She dims.
Direct hit.
Knife, puncture wound to versions unnecessary.
Because who needs a soft girl,
When mankind is unyielding?
Resistant to morality?
Might as well play with the Devil,
Sell a piece of your soul.
Selfish should rule the self,
That's her motto.
I hear her cascading thoughts,
Taunting when I get hurt.
If you cared less, you might feel more

Power
Over the weak and never succumb to
Defeat.
But if every part of me that shines
Suddenly dulls,
Who made me like that?
Just a pawn in a game?
Society leads.
She may rule in that world,
But I'd take a backseat
To the dark side of me

Journal Entry #5

Date: Redacted

Subject: Self

Mood: Overwhelmed

Trigger: Phone Call

I spent so much time preparing for impact, I don't know if I can exist in peace.

How will I learn to live in softness versus survival? The thought alone creates chaos. A war inside of me.

I yearn for the days when anxiety won't wake me. When I can have a clear mind. I wonder if it'll get easier to breathe without the pressure of the unknown. Or will the unknown follow me.

It won't be easy, but I hope it's achievable. To live in peace if only for moments. To not always have to hit the button alerting those around me I'm panicking.

I wonder if I'll be able to enter a room without apprehension. Let people see me before they see agitation.

Will my soft girl era always be a myth or can I make it reality.

I need to learn to accept and move on.

To reach a point that of equilibrium.

PART III: EQUILIBRIUM

Anxiety ⇌ Peace

I laugh to keep myself from crying
So my brain now associates
Sadness with laughter
My tears no longer drop
Replaced by smiles that appear false
But what else can I do
When life stones me with
Stress
Poor health
Death
And I am surrounded by people
Who make me feel as though I'm not doing enough
As though my words are a whisper on deaf ears
I can only laugh
God thought I was strong enough to handle this all
And not to call God an ass
But His assumptions now leave me
On the verge of a mental breakdown
My guards are shattering
My heart is heavy
Blood pours from my wounds
Wounds that life gave me

I'm hurting
And trying to numb it all with a bong
I'm getting stoned while being stoned
I need to self-medicate
For a chance to survive
I'm not strong but not weak enough to give up
I'd rather hide in a blunt
Shut my thoughts off
Escape into a book
When the world bears down on me
When life gets too chaotic
When my trials and tribulations
Feel like a test I can't pass
I peek at my neighbor
The one with the straight A's
I mimic their movements
I pretend I'm not breaking
I pretend I'm not tired
And for a second, I can breathe

Anxiety SCAMMED me!

Freeze my accounts!

Journal Entry #6

Date: Redacted

Subject: Self

Mood: Happy

Trigger:

Chemical Reaction Observed: Fulfillment

I signed up for a 5 K race today

Thought that maybe I'd give myself an excuse to train.

Learn how to outrun my thoughts.

Stay just out of the reach of my demons to where their touch would escape me.

Maybe if I start living and not just surviving, they won't have space to stay.

I'm hoping the run gives me peace but honestly just the accomplishment of signing up makes me feel stronger.

Thoughts running rampage…
Mental capacity reached…
Inhale.
Exhale.
Surrender to your inner eye.
See the hidden depths of your mind.
Harmonize your mind, body, and soul.
Create a melody,
Sung from the root chakra to the head.
Spin the wheel of light.
Let your energy be a thin line,
Connecting the pressure points of your psyche.
Balance, as you teeter along.
Release, as you stick the landing.

My mind needs a lullaby.
Soothing sounds of safety.
It needs reassurance and a gentle touch.
A reminder it's ok to be.

Can you escape the unknown behind each tree?
Animals teetering on the edge, noticing your scent,
Preying on your fears and insecurities?
The darkness pulling at your seams?
Can you see the insects?
As they hop from flower to ground
Back up to spider webs,
Tangling thoughts into a weave?
The maze of green leaves,
Gently brushing your face?
Can you feel the good in the bad?
Admire the scents of earth breath,
As wind whips through memories,
Flashbacks as dew drop,
As tears on flies' wings
Soar through the night skies?
As the forest sweeps you in?
As the early morning peak of rays
Creates pink and purple waves,
A reflection of your aura's glow?
Can you figure out your own meaning,
The truth of all you can be,

As you stand deep within the rainforest
And feelings make themselves known?
Do you feel the new presence of the conscious
You never let speak?
Before this moment,
You were dormant,
Just going through life,
Pause,
Play,
Reverse,
Resume,
Now forward on
Following a path lit by self-recognition,
Where your roots spread with each step,
Heal the life within.
Now, you've reached the canopy of expectations.
You see that there's more to the rainforest,
To the inner depths of your mind,
More journeys needed to take you out of your comfort.
So will you eat from the ground?
Will you taste the fungus as you chew,
Psilocybin interacting with your saliva's enzymes,
This key to a door
That will lead to equilibrium.

I can see the heat
Feel the orange-and-red lights flicker furiously
Against sealed eyes
I can taste the aroma of burnt ash
It rains over me
Encases me in a placenta
Nutrient-enriched womb of fire
A volcano break
Lava between Mother's Earth thighs
And delivers me to the world
Rebirth
From woman to goddess
Leaving the past
The times life went wrong
Where mistakes haunted me
Now life anew
A second chance
Where fire cleansed me of my past
I will grow as a phoenix
Aware of my spiritual purpose
My reign as goddess
I will start over

See the world for all its light

Understand that love starts with self before others

Be reborn in this time

From the flames of past lives

I will rise

And fly

Yes fly

Can peace and anxiety coexist?

I found solace in my soullessness,
Listened as the echoes of my despair
Drifted between mountains,
Fell into my pen,
Dipped their quills in my tear bank
Of words and crafted a lantern,
To lead me out the dark.
Freedom, as sweet as the nectar,
Spilling from the Tree of Life.
Words of encouragement,
Velvet to my mind,
Wrapped into the song of poetry.
I speak
My life anew,
And yet I'm not in happily ever after,
Just happily for now,
A work in progress.
I push forward every day,
To find solace in my silent moments.

Today my body believed it deserved normality.

I've come face-to-face with my trauma
A self-portrait of scars barely healed
I've relieved feelings of loneliness
Of self-hatred
I've seen the child who died early on
Watched her last breaths once again
Felt the collapsing of lungs
The shattering of my heart
The ripping of my mental state
To shreds
I've touched every shard
Cut my finger
On ragged ends
Watched blood tears drip
And I didn't know
Until that moment
How hurt I really was
Until the fear of life
Was staring me back in the eyes
I didn't realize I had been in a state of mourning
Mourning the girl who grew up too fast
And who grew up cold

Who mourned the missed opportunities
Which slipped through the gaps
Of my misconstrued thoughts
I have seen the past regressions
Of my father's mistakes
That eventually became my mistakes
And I don't blame him now
I've come to terms with the conditions
The cards I've been dealt
The contract of my life signed unwillingly
Raised by a magnificent single mother
While my dad crossed country lines of lies
And started a new family
Like I was just a first try
An attempt
To see if he could be a father
And don't get me wrong
Those memories of him
In the first couple years of my life are bliss
But that makes it hurt worse
Knowing what you had
And losing it like you wasn't as
Great an addition to his life
As he was to yours

Like your presence was a
Mere chance of luck
From a love f*ck
Only temporary
Until he found his real path
A path that did not include me
I faced obstacles because of
Trauma
But I never faced
Trauma
I hid it so well
Covered it with an
I.D.G.A.F. attitude
Trauma
Something younger me would have laughed at
But now I have come face-to-face
Mirror to self-portrait
Those scars
Barely healed
Have scar tissue build-up
Are slowly recovering

Catalyst or Buffer?
My family be both.

Le Chatelier's Principle

One added reactant and the reaction changes
The product shifts
Hopes for balance
Searches for equilibrium
It requires give-and-take
To let go but also receive
To believe that the desired reaction
Is achievable
Is within reach

Life is getting easier
The burden weighs less

Mantra

I am present

I am in love with the skin I'm in

My mind is not my prison

I am not my anxiety

I am control

I write for me
The little girl whose trauma
Riddled her silent
Trapped her tears
Teased them on the cusp of desperation
I write for all the mute screams
That still play in my head
I write to come to peace with the chaos
I write to defeat my anxiety

Healing doesn't mean anxiety will never exist again.
It means every moment won't be controlled by it, but by yourself instead.
It means learning to balance the elements, to feel the emotions.

Anxiety was my chrysalis
My protective shell
My skin hardened against the outside
I fell asleep within myself
Didn't care if I'd ever wake up
I was content
A child not wanting to grow up
But then my body started to break
Down
My mind reorganized
Neurons that had been dull
Started to fire
I began to feel
My shell began to crack
Quickly I had to adapt
Transform
Become bigger than my nervous system
It could no longer hold me back
Sleep couldn't provide me with a safe habitat
I was wide awake
Breaking free
Something deep inside of me

Was fluttering
My heartbeat
Breath was all I could hear
Breathe
Breathe
Breathe in the breeze
Freedom
Hope
Rebirth
On repeat
I felt ethereal
I shredded my fear
Felt my arms elongate
Become delicate wings
I grew stronger
A force in nature
I was nature
Living in the meadows
Blooming with the flowers
The little girl inside me
Now blossomed
Into a full-grown woman
Flying
High

Poetry gives me freedom.
Science gives me structure.

Final Experiment Report

Objective: To analyze and understand the chemical imbalance that contributes to anxiety. This goal is to bring visibility to the relationship between chemistry and our emotions.

Hypothesis: Can poetry make the invisible chemistry of anxiety visible?

Methods: Poetry, Prose, and Journal Entries

Results: Collected observations confirmed that there is a relationship between the chemistry of our body and emotions. Through poetic expressions, analyst was able to properly show the correlation between the two. Emotions are not predictable and can be brought on by the unknown. The unknown is seen to be the effect from the imbalance of chemicals.

Future Research: Future studies will examine the state of equilibrium and how reaching this point alters the mind. Analyst will further explore other emotions and bring chemical visibility to the complex nature of our mind.

Personal Reflection Log

What did this experiment reveal about you?

Acknowledgements

I want to thank everyone who has walked on this journey with me.

To my family and friends, your support and patience mean the world. Thank you for believing in me and supporting my poetry. Your love fuels me to keep going and pursue my dreams.

To every person who has battled anxiety, overthinking, and fear. You are not alone and I hope my words remind you that healing is possible.

About the Author

Nyarko, formerly known as Amzane, is a South Florida–based poet and author whose work explores the intersection of science and emotion.

Her writing invites readers to examine human experiences through both a scientific and deeply personal lens, proving that emotions can be studied just as closely as they are felt.

When she's not writing, Nyarko works in the pharmaceutical industry, where her passion for chemistry continues to inspire her creative work. She is also the author of *Soul Thoughts*.

Connect with Nyarko on social media.

IG @NyarkoThePoet
TikTok @NyarkoThePoet_
Website: www.nyarkothepoet.com

The experiment continues.

Impaired: The Chemical Truth of Grief

Coming Soon

www.ingramcontent.com/pod-product-compliance
Lightning Source LLC
LaVergne TN
LVHW050921210926
848482LV00012B/491